D1139788

GOD
ANSWERS
PRAYER

for boys

GOD ANSWERS PRAYER

PRAYER

for boys

IRENE HOWAT

CF4•K

10 9 8 7 6 5 4 3 2 1
© Copyright 2013 Christian Focus Publications
ISBN: 978-1-78191-152-5

Published by Christian Focus Publications,
Geanies House, Fearn, Tain, Ross-shire,
IV20 1TW, Scotland, U.K.
www.christianfocus.com
E-mail: info@christianfocus.com

Cover design by Daniel van Straaten
Cover illustration by Neil Reed

Character illustration by Brent Donahoe
Printed and bound by Bell and Bain, Glasgow

Scripture quotations are from the HOLY BIBLE,
NEW INTERNATIONAL VERSION®. NIV®.
Copyright©1973, 1978, 1984 by International Bible
Society. Used by permission of Zondervan.

All rights reserved. No part of this publication may be
reproduced, stored in a retrieval system, or transmitted,
in any form, by any means, electronic, mechanical,
photocopying, recording or otherwise without the prior
permission of the publisher or a licence permitting
restricted copying. In the U.K. such licences are issued
by the Copyright Licensing Agency, Saffron House, 6-10
Kirby Street, London, EC1 8TS. www.cla.co.uk

FOR
EVAN ADAM
STEWART

CONTENTS

WHO DOES WHAT?

When we want to do something, it can make us unhappy if we aren't allowed to do it and someone else is. But it didn't make King David unhappy one little bit. Here's the story.

David was king of Israel and Judah and a splendid king he was too. After defeating his enemies (and there had been plenty of them over the years!) he settled down and made Jerusalem his capital city. As kings do, he had a magnificent palace built and it became his home. That was when he had his good idea. Being a man of God, he sent for one of the Lord's prophets to tell him about his good idea. Nathan the prophet arrived at David's command and this is what the king told him.

> Here I am, living in a palace of cedar, while the ark of God remains in a tent (2 Samuel 7:2).

9

That may not make too much sense to you, but Nathan knew exactly what he meant.

The ark of the Lord was a beautiful box that had been made at God's instruction many years before. In it was a piece of the manna that the Lord had supplied to keep his people alive after they escaped from Egypt. And along with the manna there were the two stone blocks on which were written God's Ten Commandments. Over the years the ark of the Lord had been carried from place to place as God's people moved. They didn't feel safe when it wasn't with them. It had been captured by enemies but was now safely back in Jerusalem. As far as the people were concerned, all was well. However, David felt that it wasn't right that he should live in a magnificent palace made of cedar wood while the ark of the Lord was in a tent. That's when David had a good idea.

The prophet Nathan also thought it was a good idea. But that night the Lord spoke to Nathan and told him something different.

> Go and tell my servant David, 'This is what the LORD says: Are you the one to build me a house to dwell in? ... When your days are over and you rest with your fathers, I will raise up your offspring to succeed you ... and I will establish his kingdom.

He is the one who will build a house for my Name
...' (2 Samuel 7: 5, 12-13).

Nathan went back to King David and told him what God had said.

What did David do? Did he grump and say that it was his good idea to build a house for the ark of God? Did he moan that it wasn't fair that his son should do what he wanted to do himself? Did David complain to Nathan that God had favourites? No, he did not. In fact, David prayed one of the most beautiful prayers in the whole Bible.

> Who am I, O Sovereign LORD, and what is my family, that you have brought me thus far? And as if this were not enough in your sight, O Sovereign LORD, you have also spoken about the future of the house of your servant. ... Now be pleased to bless the house of your servant, that it may continue forever in your sight; for you, O Sovereign LORD, have spoken and with your blessing the house of your servant will be blessed forever (2 Samuel 7:18-19, 29).

And that's exactly what happened. In those days 'the house of your servant' meant the family of your servant. And the house, or family, of David has been blessed forever because if was from his family that the Lord Jesus Christ came.

If you look up the beginning of the Gospel of Matthew, you'll find a whole list of names. Read through them and do

11

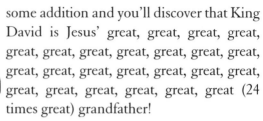

some addition and you'll discover that King David is Jesus' great, great (24 times great) grandfather!

So did David just get on with being king and leave the building of a house for the ark of God to his son Solomon? No, he didn't. He commanded those who ruled under him to come to Jerusalem and he made a speech.

> 'Listen to me,' he said. 'I had it in my heart to build a house as a place of rest for the ark of the covenant of the LORD ... and I made plans to build it. But God said to me, "You are not to build a house for my name ... Solomon your son is the one who will build my house ..."' (1 Chronicles 28:2-3, 6).

Then David gave Solomon some scrolls. They were plans he had drawn for the temple he had wanted to build! He'd even worked out the weight of gold that was needed. King David told those who ruled under him that he was providing 100 tons of gold and 240 tons of silver for the temple as well as bronze and iron and wood. Not only that, he was providing large quantities of fine stone and marble along with precious stones and specially trained workmen. That doesn't sound like a man who was annoyed with God for not letting him carry out his good idea. Nor does it sound like a dad who was jealous of his son because God was going to let him do it instead.

Years passed, King David died and Solomon his son became king after him. God kept his word and Solomon was able to use his dad's plans, his silver and gold, stone, marble and ideas to build the most magnificent temple for the ark of God. It became the centre of worship for the Jewish people for hundreds of years.

When the temple was completed, King Solomon made a speech and we even know the words he used. Reading them shows us something about Solomon. Although God gave him the privilege of building the temple, Solomon freely admitted that the good idea wasn't his, but his dad's.

> My father David had it in his heart to build a temple for the Name of the LORD … The LORD has kept the promise he made, I have succeeded David my father and now I sit on the throne of Israel, just as the LORD promised, and I have built the temple for the Name of the LORD, the God of Israel (1 Kings 8:18, 20).

After he finished speaking to the people, Solomon prayed a long prayer to God. At the end of it he said, 'Now arise, O Lord God, and come to your resting place, you and the ark of your might.'

Animals had been killed and laid out in the temple as sacrifices to God. When Solomon finished his prayer, God sent fire from heaven to burn up the sacrifices and the glory of God filled the temple. Solomon must have known for sure that he and his father had done the right thing.

When David and Solomon prayed, they remembered how great God is and worshipped him. When we pray we shouldn't just come to the Lord with 'shopping lists' of things we want; we should remember who he is, who we are, and worship him for being so great.

FOR US

It was early in the morning when the man got up. He left the house he was staying in and found a quiet place away from anyone else. Yesterday had been such a busy day. Let's find out what happened.

In the morning he and his friends had gone to worship God. The man had taught those who were gathered there. The people were amazed because he spoke differently from their usual teachers. It wasn't that he had a strange accent, or anything like that, it was that he had power in his words. But the service was interrupted by a man shouting out!

'What do you want with us, Jesus of Nazareth?' the man yelled. 'Have you come to destroy us? I know who you are – the Holy One of God!'

You've guessed! The teacher was Jesus.

Everyone watched to see what he would do.

'Be quiet!' Jesus said firmly. 'Come out of him!'

It hadn't been the man speaking at all. It was an evil spirit inside him that had shouted out! Because Jesus has power over all things the evil spirit had to obey his command. Screeching as he went, the spirit shook the poor man and then left him.

Just imagine what the people in the synagogue thought of that!

'What's this?' they asked each other.

They started to talk about Jesus. News about what had happened spread like wildfire all round Galilee.

But that's not all that happened that day. After they had worshipped God, Jesus went to Simon Peter and Andrew's home. Peter is the more usual name for Simon Peter and that's what we'll call him. Peter's mother-in-law was ill. She had a high temperature and was feeling very poorly. When Jesus arrived at the house he went through to see her, took her hand and helped her up. An amazing thing happened. The fever went away immediately! Do you know what it's like after you've had a high temperature? You feel yucky for a while before you're really better. Well, Peter's mother-in-law was completely better right away. Jesus had miraculously healed her. She felt so well that she served dinner to the family and to Jesus.

And that's not all that happened that day! After sunset, just when Jesus would have been feeling like going to bed, people started coming to the door of the house where he was staying. Men and women who were sick and some who had evil spirits came to see him. They had heard about what had happened. How tired Jesus must have been. However, he healed those who were ill and drove the evil spirits out of the people they were troubling and that was the end of a long … long … day for Jesus.

The next morning, when he might still have been in bed sound asleep, Jesus got up again and left for a private place. Why? He went there to pray. Jesus, who came down from heaven to save us from our sins, wanted to spend time in the quiet of the morning with his Father in heaven. And if Jesus wanted to do that, we should too because God is the heavenly Father of all who believe in him.

Boys and girls who live in happy homes love spending time with their dads. Sadly, not every home is happy, there's not a dad in every home and not every dad is kind to his children. But God, our heavenly Father, is absolutely good, absolutely loving. He loves his people so much that he sent his one and only Son to die on the cross so that those who trust in him can go home to heaven when they die. And his one and only Son is Jesus. No wonder Jesus wanted to spend time with his Father.

When you have to decide something important, do you talk it over with your dad? When Jesus was going to choose who should be his special friends he found another quiet place and spent time there praying to his Father.

As you grow older you'll find you have to make more and more decisions. It is always good to talk to a caring adult, but remember to talk to your Father in heaven too.

There is another of Jesus' prayers that we can read in the Bible. And in this prayer he was praying for us! Jesus prayed to his Father in heaven for all the people who would believe in him throughout history, right up to the time when Jesus finally returns.

Now here's something to be very, very thankful for. You know that Jesus went to heaven after he rose from the dead. But I wonder if you know what he is doing there? Well, the Bible tells us that he is still praying. Jesus is praying to his Father in heaven for all those who have asked him to forgive their sins and to be their Saviour. Isn't it an amazing thing that Jesus our Saviour, who died for us on the cross, still loves us so much that he's praying for us even now? What a Saviour!

THE DESPERATE DAD

When Jesus was on earth, news of his miracles passed from person to person, village to village and town to town. This happened long before the telephone, television and the Internet!

In a town in Galilee there lived a man called Jairus. He was an important man in the community because he was one of the rulers in the synagogue. Synagogues were rather like churches today but they were also a bit like local authority offices too. Everyone in the town would have known and respected Jairus. He was also a dad. He may have had several children, but the only one we know about was a girl who, at the time of this story was twelve years old.

However, Jairus' daughter was critically ill and her father was very worried about her.

We don't know if she'd taken ill suddenly or if she'd been unwell for months, or even years. All we

know for sure is that the end was near and Jairus was desperate to do anything he could to help the daughter he loved.

News arrived in the town that Jesus, who had a reputation for healing people, was on his way. Apparently he had been on the other side of the lake and was about to arrive by boat. Jairus rushed to the lakeside. Imagine his impatience as the little boat was rowed towards the shore. Time was running out for his child.

Jesus was no sooner out of the boat when Jairus threw himself at his feet.

'My little daughter is dying. Please come and put your hands on her so that she will be healed and live.'

Of course Jairus was speaking to Jesus face to face, but that was still prayer. Prayer is speaking to God and Jesus is God!

Jesus understood right away that the need was urgent and he set out with Jairus towards his house. A large crowd followed the two men, pushing in on them. No doubt they wanted to hear what Jesus was saying and see what he was doing. Crowds like to know all that's going on!

Then a strange thing happened. A little way ahead Jesus stopped walking, turned round and asked who had touched him. Jairus must have been very confused, not to say worried. Dozens of people were touching Jesus! If he was going to stop and speak to every one of them, his daughter would be dead by the time they got to her. Eventually an ill-looking woman stepped forward and admitted that she had touched Jesus. The Lord then questioned her and her story poured out. She had been ill for twelve years and had reached out to touch Jesus' clothes in the belief that she would be healed. And she was!

This all took much longer to happen than it has taken you to read about it. The woman was probably shy and embarrassed and it took time for her to admit what had happened. Poor Jairus! He must have been frantic with fear. Then he looked towards his home and saw some men coming. Their faces were sad for they had terrible news to tell.

'Your daughter is dead,' they said to Jairus. 'Why bother the teacher any more?'

What dreadful news.

Jesus looked at Jairus and told him, 'Don't be afraid; just believe.'

Ignoring the messengers, Jairus rushed towards his home, Jesus beside him. It must have been so hard, but he believed that Jesus could still do something wonderful.

At that time in that country paid mourners were hired to weep and wail when someone died, and those who knew the family joined in the weeping and wailing. It was their way of showing how

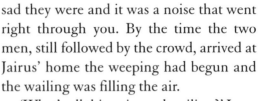

sad they were and it was a noise that went right through you. By the time the two men, still followed by the crowd, arrived at Jairus' home the weeping had begun and the wailing was filling the air.

'What's all this noise and wailing?' Jesus asked. 'The child is not dead but asleep.'

The wailing turned to laughing – a horrible kind of laughter that mocked Jesus.

Jesus put all the noisy people out of the house and took his friends Peter, James and John, along with the girl's parents, and went inside. Jairus' daughter was lying there dead. When Jesus said that she was sleeping, he meant he was going to waken her up from the dead. Only he can do that for he is God and it is God who gives life. Jairus and his wife watched Jesus as he took the dead girl's hand. Looking down on her body he spoke to her in Aramaic.

'Talitha koum,' he said, and that means, 'Little girl, I say to you, get up!'

Immediately the girl stood up and walked around the room. Her father and mother were astonished. Peter, James and John were astonished too. And no wonder; it was an absolutely astonishing thing to do, to raise a dead girl to life again!

'Don't let anyone know about this,' Jesus told Jairus and his wife. 'And give her something to eat.'

That must have been the happiest meal Mrs Jairus had ever made in all of her life!

There are different kinds of prayer. When Jairus fell at Jesus' feet at the lakeside, he was asking a 'Please' prayer. He desperately wanted Jesus to do something for him, to heal his dying daughter. After the Lord brought the girl back to life once again, no doubt Jairus prayed a different kind of prayer, a 'Thank-you' prayer to Jesus. I wonder if we all remember to pray a 'Thank-you' prayer when Jesus has answered one of our 'Please' prayers.

That's something to think about.

GO ON, ASK HIM

Mrs Zebedee was a fisherman's wife and she had two sons. She may have had other children as well, but we don't know about them. Her sons were called James and John and they were alive at the time of Jesus. Imagine her surprise one day when her husband came home from work and told her what had happened.

'I was down on the beach with the boys,' (parents always call their sons 'boys' and their daughters 'girls' even when they are grown up!) and Jesus, the wandering preacher, came along. Peter and Andrew were with him.'

Mrs Zebedee knew Peter and Andrew as they too were from a local fishing family.

'Well,' her husband continued, 'Jesus looked at James and John and then told them to follow him.'

'What did they do?' she must have asked.

Zebedee shook his head. 'They got up from the nets and went with him. I was left alone with a whole pile of nets to mend myself. It took me three times longer than usual to sort them.'

'It would,' she agreed, 'because the work is usually divided among the three of you.'

No doubt the couple sat and talked about what had happened, wondering if James and John would be back fishing in a day or two after their interest in Jesus had passed. If that's what they thought, they were very much mistaken. Their two sons became members of the small group of men who followed Jesus, learning from what he said and did. Jesus had twelve close friends who spent the next three years with him. They were called his disciples. Because Jesus never travelled very far by modern day standards, Zebedee and his wife would know what was happening with James and John and would see them regularly.

Some time later, Zebedee's wife decided the time had come to talk to Jesus about something she and her sons really wanted him to do. For us, prayer means closing our eyes and speaking to God. But for her, because Jesus is God, it meant going and speaking to Jesus face to face.

'I want to ask you a favour,' she said to Jesus.

'What is it you want?' Jesus asked.

James and John's mother knew exactly what she wanted.

'Grant that one of these two sons of mine may sit at your right hand and the other at your left in your kingdom.'

Jesus looked at her. 'You don't know what you are asking,' he said to James and John, because he knew their mother was speaking on their behalf. 'Can you drink the cup I am going to drink?' Jesus asked them.

'We can,' they answered, not realising that Jesus was talking about his death.

'You will indeed drink from my cup,' he told the two young men, 'but to sit at my right or left is not for me to grant. These places belong to those for whom they have been prepared by my Father.'

Of course, the other ten disciples were not best pleased with James and John. Why should the brothers get special treatment in Jesus' kingdom? The Lord saw the argument that was brewing and used it as an opportunity to teach his disciples a lesson. He reminded them of how their rulers liked power, enjoyed telling people what to do and seeing them do it right away. Then he explained that his followers are to be different. They have to be humble rather than proud, to serve rather than be served, and he finished by telling them that some would even have to serve him by laying down their lives.

If Zebedee's wife was still standing close by when Jesus said this to his disciples, she would not have been a happy woman. She probably thought that Jesus was going to set up a kingdom on earth and that her sons would live with him in his palace and rule the country. It must have come as a shock to her to learn that her sons were being trained to be servants, and that they might even have to die because of serving Jesus.

James and John sent their mother with a prayer to Jesus, but what they wanted her to ask for was not what God wanted them to have. God hears and answers all prayers and the answer to her prayer was 'No'. When we pray for things that God doesn't want us to have, he hears our prayers and answers them, and his answer to us is 'No', because God always knows and does what is best for his people.

THE UNTOUCHABLE MAN

Perhaps you've had chickenpox or some other disease that brought you out in a rash. If you have, you were probably kept away from other children in order to prevent them catching it. Not so very long ago parents took a different approach. If they heard about a child nearby who had an illness like chickenpox, they used to take their son or daughter to play with the poorly neighbour so that their child caught the illness while they were still young. That might seem a cruel thing to do, but there was some sense it in because children tend to get better from these things more quickly than grown-ups.

Long ago, when Jesus was on earth, there was a disease that everyone feared. And they certainly didn't allow their child to play with someone who suffered from it. The disease was known as leprosy. It started out with a patch on the skin and then it

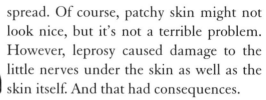

spread. Of course, patchy skin might not look nice, but it's not a terrible problem. However, leprosy caused damage to the little nerves under the skin as well as the skin itself. And that had consequences.

Imagine that you have a patch on your foot and the nerves around it become damaged. You then have an area of foot that doesn't feel heat or cold or pain. So you could stand on a dirty nail and not feel it. You would only know you had hurt yourself when the wound became infected, or if you noticed blood on your socks. If that happened today, you would be given an antibiotic and the nurse would put dressings on your foot until the wound healed and you were better again.

In Jesus' day there was no suitable medicine and nerves damaged by leprosy were really bad news. Sufferers accidentally hurt themselves so often and so much that their feet became badly damaged until they couldn't walk. Their hands and fingers became useless stumps! It was a horrible disease. Even today in parts of the poor world people suffer from an illness quite like this. Thankfully there are now medicines to cure it if it is caught early, and operations that can help mend hands and feet.

At the time Jesus lived on earth, people with leprosy were made to leave their homes and families.

They had to live with other sufferers like themselves. What a terrible thing it was to suffer from leprosy. Nobody would hold your hand again. Nobody would give you a hug. You would feel dirty. In fact, sufferers from leprosy were told to shout, 'Unclean! Unclean!' when people came near, to warn them of the danger.

One day a man who was suffering from leprosy knelt down before Jesus. How surprising it must have been when Jesus didn't run away like other people.

The poor man prayed to Jesus. 'Lord,' he said, 'if you are willing, you can make me clean.'

That was an amazing prayer. There was no cure for leprosy, but the man believed that Jesus was powerful enough to do what no doctor could do and what no medicine could do. Then an amazing thing happened. Jesus reached out his hand and touched the man! He must have been absolutely astounded!

Having touched the poor leprous man, Jesus then spoke to him.

'I am willing,' the Lord said, 'Be clean!'

Jesus commanded the leprosy to go away ... and it did! Immediately the man was cured! Imagine how he felt. He would want to run and jump, to go from person to person telling them he was better. He'd want to find his family and show them

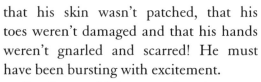

that his skin wasn't patched, that his toes weren't damaged and that his hands weren't gnarled and scarred! He must have been bursting with excitement.

But Jesus told the man that there was something he had to do before he set out to find his family and friends.

> See, that you don't tell anyone. But go, show yourself to the priest and offer the gift Moses commanded (Matthew 8:4).

Why did the Lord tell him to do such a strange thing? In the Old Testament Law that God gave to his people, there were rules to do with health. One of them was about people who once had leprosy and who became better – a very unusual happening. They had to go to the priest who would examine them to see that they really were well. Then the person who had been cured would give an offering to God that would be sacrificed by the priest. After that he was declared clean and was able to go back to his home and family.

That was why Jesus told the man to go to the priest. When the priest had examined him people would be in no doubt at all that he was completely healed. The offering was a way of thanking God for the healing and also asking for forgiveness of sins.

Did the man do exactly what Jesus told him? If you had been healed from a terrible disease, wouldn't you have obeyed the person who healed you? Well, instead of going quietly to the priest, the man told *everyone* what had happened. Before long news spread that Jesus had healed a man from leprosy. It was amazing! It was astounding! People wanted to see this miracle-worker; they wanted to catch a glimpse of the one who could cure leprosy. Crowds gathered round Jesus and prevented him from going into the nearby towns. By not doing as the Lord told him the man who had been healed actually caused difficulties for the very person he most wanted to thank.

Those who trust in Jesus have been healed from the worst disease of all, from sin-sickness. Our sins have been washed away. Jesus tells us, 'Go and sin no more.' The sad thing is that we, just like that man, often don't do what Jesus tells us. But we can always ask the Lord for forgiveness. Remember the leper's prayer: 'Lord if you are willing, you can make me clean.'

Jesus always hears and answers that prayer, if it is prayed from the heart.

WHAT NOT TO ASK

Meet Augustine. He's just the kind of boy you don't want to be. For example, he tells lies. He tells lies because he has a vivid imagination and can make up splendid stories. He tells lies to get himself out of trouble when he has done wrong and is about to be found out. Augustine tells lies because it makes him feel smarter than other boys. And he tells lies just because he likes it. Does he sound like someone you might know?

Here's a little more about Augustine. He's a thief. He steals from his parents, taking food that he's not meant to have and other things too. Stealing is a game he likes playing. Once again it makes him feel smart. He's outwitting people and not being found out. He could be just like someone from your street or school.

Before he is twelve years old Augustine drinks alcohol. Not only that, but he steals the wine from his dad's cellar. And to make matters even worse he

sometimes gives drink to his friends who, no doubt, are about the same age as he is.

Although Augustine sounds like a real twenty-first century boy – the kind your folks don't want you to have as a friend – he was actually born in AD 354 in North Africa, that's over 1,700 years ago! Knowing when he lived explains his subjects at school. He studied Latin and loved it. Latin lessons were full of battles and wars, of love stories and heroes, and Roman gods – who were just idols. Augustine also learned Greek, but hated it as these lessons were hard work and not very interesting at all. However, overall Augustine was a very clever boy and did well at school.

Patricius, his dad, believed in the Roman idol gods and worshipped them. His mother, Monica, was a Christian and she prayed to the one true God for her son. How he needed her prayers! Mothers know things that their children don't know that they know. Read that last sentence again and think about it! She knew what Augustine was like. Monica knew he was often in trouble, that he told lies and much else besides.

When he was about sixteen years old Augustine did something really stupid. Picture the scene. It was late autumn and there was a pear tree covered with fruit. Augustine stripped all the pears off the tree and fed them to pigs in a nearby field! That pear tree belonged to someone else; that made him a thief. But what he did was just mindless destruction. It's like someone today breaking windows or throwing bricks from a bridge on to cars below. That was Augustine.

Monica had taught Augustine to pray to God and from time to time he did just that. But he prayed the kind of prayer that God doesn't want to hear. His prayers sounded something like this. 'I know I've been a liar, God, but please don't let me be found out. I don't want to get into trouble.' 'I know I shouldn't have taken the wine from Dad's cellar, but please don't let him find out. Let him think it was the servant girl who drank it.' 'I know I shouldn't have stolen the pears and fed them to the pigs, Lord. Please let the man think it was someone else and not know it was me.' He wasn't interested in asking God to forgive him. Augustine just didn't want to be punished!

Augustine's life went from bad to worse through his teens and twenties. As a student he did things you wouldn't want to read about. And all the time his mother prayed for him. Monica knew that God hears and answers prayer and she just kept on praying, weeping and praying for her son who had gone so terribly wrong.

From time to time Augustine's conscience troubled him. He knew about God and sometimes even prayed to him and tried to live a better life. One day, Augustine prayed something like this. 'Lord, help me

to live a clean life and to keep it up ... but not yet.' Imagine that! He wanted God to agree that he should keep on sinning until a future date when he would change and be good! Actually, we all do that sometimes. We ask God to forgive us, but don't really intend to change. God doesn't like it one little bit when we pray that kind of prayer. In fact, it's not a prayer at all; it's an insult to God and a very serious thing.

Eventually Monica's prayers were answered and Augustine and a friend believed in Jesus on the very same day. Monica was thrilled! The words are old-fashioned, but here is how Augustine described what happened after he and his friend were converted. 'Thence we go in to my mother; we tell her; she rejoiceth; we relate in order how it took place; she exulteth, and triumpheth, and Blessed God.'

Amazingly, God used Augustine in a wonderful way and he became one of the most important teachers in the early church. He had been well-known amongst the clever people of his day and when they saw the difference God made in his life, they were amazed. Then when people started teaching things that were not in the Bible, and causing terrible trouble in the church, Augustine was clever enough to work out what was true and to help sort out the problems.

What a wonderful answer to Monica's prayers. What a wonderful God we have.

PATCHED BREECHES

In the 1960s it was common for Scottish children to have patches on their clothes. In fact, mothers seeing a child with a patched jacket would admire how well the patching had been done rather than think the child was badly dressed. One of the places that needed patching most often was the elbows of jerseys and cardigans that had been worn through by being leant on at school.

There was a Scotsman in the sixteenth century who had a reputation for wearing holes in his clothes. But the holes weren't on his elbows. Rather they were on the knees of his breeches because he'd spent so many hours on his knees in prayer. Now, if you don't know what breeches were, they were thick hard-wearing trousers and quite common in the sixteenth century.

The man's name was John Welch[1] but nobody who knew him as a teenager would have thought he would ever have worn through his breeches by praying! Born in Scotland in 1568, there were few things John enjoyed better as a boy than playing truant from school with his friends. Unfortunately he became a member of a gang on the borderland between Scotland and England. The gang was bad news because they were thieves and robbers and they raided homes on both sides of the border.

It is a fact that money easily come by is money easily lost and John found that out for himself. He had money after he and his friends had stolen it, but it seemed to just disappear for he never had anything to show for it. In fact, he ended up with no money and no true friends. But God used that bad time to show John the love of Jesus. John Welch realised what an awful life he was leading and became a Christian.

Mr Welch, John's father, was gracious enough to forgive his son despite the pain and heartbreak he had caused. And he must have been pleased to see young John heading off for Edinburgh University to study to be a minister. At the end of John's training it was back to the Borders when he became minister of

---

[1] Welch is pronounced Welsh.

Selkirk in 1588. He spent hours in prayer each day and night. In fact he slept very little. Each night he would wake up after a few hours, wrap himself in his plaid[2] and pray again until morning. John moved from Selkirk to Kirkcudbright before becoming minister in Ayr, in the southwest of Scotland. His house was just off the High Street and there was a garden there. That was where John got the reputation for wearing through the knees of his breeches. He also had a reputation for making Ayr a safer place to live. When fights broke out on the street, as they did from time to time, the minister would put on a helmet to protect himself and then rush into the middle of the brawl and stop the combatants fighting. Having taken the heat out of the situation, he would call for his wife and the woman who helped her in the house to bring food out into the street for those who had been fighting. Then, after singing a psalm with them and praying, he settled them down to a meal!

The High Street in Ayr at that time was filthy. Rubbish gathered on either side of the road, toilets didn't exist and chamber pots were emptied into the street for the rain to wash away the contents. I won't

---

[2] A plaid is somewhere between a rug and a blanket and it was what Scots wrapped round themselves in the days before coats became common.

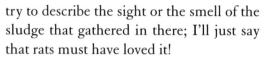

try to describe the sight or the smell of the sludge that gathered in there; I'll just say that rats must have loved it!

In 1604 rumours began to arrive in Ayr that the plague had reached Scotland. The news struck terror in people's hearts. When the plague reached a town it spread like wildfire from family to family, from street to street. In fact, it spread wherever rats could scurry for they caught and carried the disease. Tradesmen and travellers brought news that the plague had arrived on the east coast of Scotland and it was travelling relentlessly westwards.

Ayr people, there were about 3,000 of them, heard their minister on the subject and he didn't take the matter lightly. Yes, the plague was likely to come, he told them. Yes, many of them might die. And yes, God would forgive their sins and take them home to heaven, if they confessed and believed in the Lord Jesus. But the good John Welch didn't only preach, he also prayed and the people knew it.

One day two pedlars arrived at the bottom of the cobbles leading up to the Auld Brig over the River Ayr. They wanted into the town to sell what they were carrying. That was how trade was done in those days and it was nothing unusual. But the plague had made men wary and the town baillie[3] sent for John Welch. When the minister arrived he listened to the pedlars' request and then prayed to God. Believing that his heavenly Father was guiding him, he said, 'Baillie, cause these men to put on their packs again and be gone; for if God be in heaven, the plague is in these sacks.' The two men, who looked quite healthy, lifted up their sacks and left Ayr behind them.

The pedlars decided to go to Cumnock, just sixteen miles away. But John Welch was right, they did carry the plague and the poor town of Cumnock suffered an outbreak that cost many lives. The people of Ayr knew they had been spared because their godly minister was a man of prayer and some trusted in the Lord Jesus as a result.

We can see that prayer for John Welch wasn't just a few words to God each morning and evening, it was a way of life. It can be our way of life too and what a difference that would make.

---

[3] Civic officer in the local government of Scotland.

NOT SHORT AND SNAPPY

If you want someone to read what you've written, you give it an interesting title. For example, would you choose a book called 'The Daring Adventure' or one called 'What happened on Saturday when we went down to the shore to the north of the headland at Westsea'? You might find it difficult to get all of the second title on to one page!

There was a man who lived in England in the eighteenth century and he wrote a leaflet with a very long name. But before you discover the name, you need to know a little about William Romaine. He was born in Hartlepool in 1714, the son of a Christian who had escaped from France when some of those who believed in Jesus were being given a very hard time. There were five children in the family, two boys and three girls.

William was a very clever young man and went off to study at Oxford University. He paid much

more attention to his books than he did to his clothes, so much so that fussy people thought he was a disgrace.

'Who is that slovenly (untidy) person with his stockings down?' someone asked, when they saw him in Oxford.

'That slovenly person, as you call him, is one of the greatest geniuses of the age, and is likely to be one of the greatest men in the kingdom,' the Master of an Oxford college replied.

You won't be at all surprised to learn that William wrote very clever books while still a young man.

Some years later William became a college lecturer as well as a minister and that was what took him to London. While he was in that great city news broke of a terrible tragedy in Portugal. An earthquake measuring 8.5 to 9 on the Richter Scale hit Lisbon almost destroying the city. The earthquake, with its epicentre under the Atlantic Ocean, was followed by a tsunami that engulfed Lisbon harbour and town before forcing its way up the Tagus River with more power than you can imagine. Men on horseback galloped as fast as they possibly could in front of the oncoming tsunami to save themselves from being washed into it and then hauled into the sea by its drag-back. After-shocks were felt as far north as Finland and as far south as

North Africa. Londoners felt two great rumbles that caused panic in the city.

When news of the earthquake and tsunami reached London people began to fear that the same thing might happen to them. Knowing the geography of England, they could envisage an earthquake with its epicentre off the southeast coast sending a tsunami right up the River Thames and washing London completely away. Thousands of people took themselves to Hyde Park thinking that was the safest place to be as there were no buildings to crash down on them. The Bishop of London called on ministers to preach to their people about the danger of dying without faith in Jesus. But William Romaine was in there first. He preached two sermons and had them printed and distributed. He also prayed, not only that England would be spared a terrible earthquake, but that people would believe in Jesus.

William wrote a booklet for his fellow ministers – and this is the one with the long title. It was called, 'An earnest Invitation to the Friends of the Established Church to join with several of their brethren, clergy and laity, in London, in setting apart an hour of every week for Prayer and Supplication during the present troublesome times.' Not exactly short and snappy!

But the problem wasn't just the earthquake. The church was in a mess. Many ministers were only preaching about the parts of the Bible they liked and their churches had fewer and fewer people going to services. Some were even jealous of preachers who were more popular because they taught their people about the Lord Jesus. You'll find it difficult to believe what happened to William Romaine. Lots of people came to hear him preach. However, he lost his job as minister because some of his congregation complained that it wasn't 'convenient' to have that number in church! You may need to read that paragraph again to take in such nonsense!

William believed that the Bible is the Word of God and tried as best he could to do what was taught in it. Jesus encouraged his followers to pray, not only alone, but to gather together to pray. What William Romaine was doing by writing his Earnest Invitation (let's give it a short name) was to get ministers and others to pray together, maybe not in the same room, but all promising to pray for an hour every week about the troubles, both in the church and in the world. Did anyone accept his invitation? Yes, they did. About twelve ministers wrote to William from different parts of England saying that they would join in his scheme. But one by one others were added until over

300 men, ministers and others, were making time for one hour of prayer each week for England.

Prayer was very much part of life and William made sure that was true for his family and servants too. William started his day with prayer and then had breakfast at 6 am. At 9 am his family and servants gathered for a time of Bible reading and prayer. From 10 am until lunchtime William visited the people in his church, reading the Bible and praying in each home. Half past one was dinnertime, after which he studied and, yes – you've guessed – he prayed. Supper was served at 7 pm and then William often went for a walk, especially in the summer. At 9 pm the family and servants all met once again for Bible reading and prayer before he went off to bed at 10 o'clock prompt!

How do I know William Romaine's daily timetable over 250 years later? Well, he was so strict about keeping to it that several people noted it down in their diaries!

So, because of these scribbles, we know that not only did William pray himself, but he encouraged others to do so to. I wonder if we ever do that.

THE TEN YEAR
SILENCE

John Berridge, an English farmer's son, was born in 1716. He had three younger brothers, some of whom might have been interested in farming. John certainly was not. It may be that part of the reason for his lack of interest was that he lived with an aunt in Nottingham for much of his childhood. He was quite a serious lad, but not half as serious as a boy who lived near his aunt, and whose house he passed each day as he went to school.

One day, as he was walking to his aunt's house after school, the other boy stopped him.

'May I read to you out of the Bible?' John was asked.

Not wanting to be rude, he agreed to listen. He wasn't best pleased about it, but he was even less pleased when his friend seemed to think that every time John passed his door he should have the Bible read to him! As day followed day this began to annoy John. And, of course, if you allow something to annoy you, you just become more and more annoyed. That's exactly what happened.

The problem was that people knew what was going on and John developed a reputation for being religious – which he was not. One day the school was on holiday and John spent the day at a fair. Don't think of a fair as roundabouts, exciting rides and amusement arcades! Fairs in those days were about sheep and cows, apples and barley and about people bringing things they had grown or made to be sold. But it was all good fun because it was a holiday.

On his way home John drew near to the other boy's house and he dreaded passing it in case he was caught. He'd had such a good day and the last thing he wanted was to sit and listen to chapters of the Bible being read to him. But the boy was watching out and pounced on John as he drew near his door.

'Would you like to come in and read the Bible?' he asked. Then, without waiting for an answer, he added, 'and we could pray together.'

John wished he was back at the fair! But he had no choice but to go inside.

After John left his friend it bothered his conscience that he felt so mean when this boy was trying to help him. So he decided that he should be as religious as his young friend. Following his example, he started inviting his friends into his aunt's home and offering to read the Bible and pray with them. At least he understood how embarrassed they were! But his enthusiasm for religion wore off quite soon and his friends were able to enjoy themselves with John once again.

At the age of fourteen John left school and went back home to the farm. He was not in the least bothered about sheep. He couldn't have cared less about the price of cattle. And pigs held no interest for him whatsoever. Mr Berridge decided to take him to the market, thinking that would spark an interest in farming as a career. Nothing sparked at all!

'John,' said his father one day in exasperation, 'I shall have to send you to college to be a minister.'

You see, John still had the reputation of being religious, but religious does not always mean Christian.

It was to the famous university in Cambridge that John went to study in 1754, leaving his father to try to persuade his younger brothers to become farmers. John was nineteen years old. Nine years later he became a minister so he must have been religious. Or was he? After some time John Berridge admitted to a most peculiar thing. He said that for ten whole years, before he was a minister and even after that, he never, ever prayed! He read the Bible. He meditated (thought deeply) about what he read in the Bible, but he didn't speak to God in prayer. And if you think that is very, very odd, you are absolutely right.

From Cambridge John went to two different churches. It won't surprise you that he didn't see people coming to faith in Jesus. Who could learn from a minister who didn't pray? John's problem was that he believed that people who tried very hard to be good could make themselves good enough to go to heaven. This is not something that John read in God's Word. The Bible says clearly that we are all sinners and the only way any of us can go to heaven is by confessing our sins to God and asking the Lord Jesus to be our Saviour.

In 1757 John realised that he wasn't a successful minister at all. That began to trouble him deeply. One day, while he was thinking about a verse of the Bible (notice that he was thinking about it rather than praying!) some words came into his mind. He said that they came like a dart from heaven. The words were, 'Cease from thine own works; only believe.' Suddenly John knew that he was wrong. His own good works couldn't save him, he had only to believe in Jesus. From then on he was a different man. He read the Bible differently.

He thought differently. And he prayed … that was certainly different!

After that he became a different kind of minister too. He preached sermons people could understand and men and women became Christians. John decided to preach outside of his own church even though that wasn't approved of at the time. So he became like a missionary, even preaching about the Lord Jesus at open air meetings. His diary tells of the very first time he did that.

Along with another man 'we called at a farmhouse. … I went into the yard, and seeing nearly a hundred and fifty people, I called for a table, and preached for the first time in the open air. Then we went to Meldred, where I preached in a field to about four thousand people. … Here the presence of the Lord was wonderfully among us.'

Had John Berridge written down some of the lessons he had learned, this might have been a quote from his diary. 'I've learned that you can be religious without being Christian. And I've learned that you can't be a Christian and not pray.'

From time to time every Christian finds it hard to pray, but the secret of praying is … to keep praying.

BACKWARDS AND FORWARDS

George Müller started off life in Prussia, which is now part of Germany. Most boys are interested in what they can do but George was more interested in what he could get. He liked money and he didn't mind how he got it. In fact, while he was still a small boy he used to steal from his father who kept work money at home. On one occasion George took some of his father's money and hid it in his shoe, thinking that was a very clever thing to do. But George's father was even more clever and he found the coins.

You might have thought that after this George would have learned his lesson, but he was the kind of boy who didn't learn lessons easily. As he grew up through his teens he went from bad to worse and once again money was part of the problem. As well as stealing from his father, he stole from other people too. Once, when he stayed in a guest house in 1821,

he escaped out the window rather than pay the bill! That was such a bad idea that he landed in prison as a result. The terrible thing is that he was just sixteen years old!

Stealing and cheating weren't George's only ways of getting cash for himself; he also gambled and won money from his friends – who didn't stay friends with him for very long. Had you met George Müller when he was sixteen years old you would have thought he was a bad lot heading for a bad life and that he would finish by spending most of it behind bars. And you would have been seriously wrong!

George became a Christian and, in 1828, he moved from Prussia to England. Not long afterwards he heard a preacher saying that God provides all the needs of his people. Taking that quite literally, George decided that he would work for no money and expect God to provide all he needed. What a turnaround! From a thief who stole money, God changed George into a missionary who refused any pay!

It wasn't that George Müller didn't need money over the years, he did … lots of it. For God called him to do a special job. At that time in Bristol, England, there was a terrible outbreak of a disease called cholera. It spread quickly from street to street through the city and left many people dead. Sadly, it also left many children with no parents to care for them and no homes to live in. Street children are not new in the twenty-first century; there were plenty of them in Bristol in the early 1830s.

Along with another preacher called Henry Craik, George set up orphan homes in Bristol, places where children were cared for, taught trades that would help them to make their own way in the world and learned about the Lord Jesus Christ. Now, it would have been just wonderful if God had used George and Henry to look after ten or twenty Bristol street children, but the amazing thing is that by 1870 there was room for over 2,000 children in five different orphan homes. Imagine how much that cost!

How do you think George Müller and Henry Craik had enough money to do what they did? Do you think they advertised the orphan work and asked for donations? No, they didn't do that. Do you think they asked other preachers to tell their church members how many children were being cared for? No, they didn't do that either. And they certainly did not write about the money they needed in the Bristol newspaper, hoping that rich people would give them thousands of pounds. The only person George and Henry told about what they needed was God and he never once let them down.

That's not to say that they didn't have times when it looked as though there wasn't going to be enough. On many occasions the children were sitting down to a meal not knowing that George and Henry were in another room telling God that there was no food to put on the tables. And remember, there were hundreds of children! But never, not once, did they have to go to bed hungry. God always sent someone with enough food or enough money.

One morning there wasn't food for the children's breakfast and George went to God in prayer and told him the seriousness of the situation. Shortly afterwards a man came to the door and handed in enough money to buy breakfast for every one of the children! That was wonderful, but the story behind that donation is more wonderful still and even George Müller didn't know about it for several months.

George mentioned what had happened that morning in the annual report. The man who gave the donation read the report and then arrived on George's doorstep to tell him this story.

'I was going to my work in Bristol early that morning when a thought came into my head. I will go to Mr Müller's orphan house and give them a donation. So I turned round and walked about a quarter of a mile towards the orphanage. Then I thought to myself that I was being foolish neglecting my work. I could give my donation another time. So I turned round again and set off towards work.'

The man continued. 'As I walked back towards my work, I thought once again to myself. The orphans may need my money right now and they might not have enough if I don't take it to them right away. So I turned round yet again and walked all the way to the orphan home and handed in the money.'

'Which was used immediately to buy bread and milk for the children,' George said, knowing that he had been praying when the man was walking backward and forward between his work and the orphan home. God had heard and answered his prayers – as he always did.

Sometimes there were more urgent needs than money. Once, George Müller prayed for a biting cold wind to stop blowing, and it did! The orphan home was heated by a large furnace that needed a big repair. Had the repair been needed in the summer that wouldn't have been a problem, but it was winter. It was freezing cold and a fierce wind was blowing which made it even colder. The children knew that the furnace wasn't working properly so George asked them to pray for two things. The first was that God would stop a storm

coming and the second was that the repair men would do the work quickly and well.

The children prayed and watched and waited for God to answer. For five days before the furnace had to be shut down for repair, the wind blew and there was snow in the air. Then, when the day came for the work to be started, the boys and girls woke up to sunshine and a day that felt like early spring! They knew that their first prayer had been answered, but they kept praying their second prayer. Knowing that the cold weather could come back at any time, the workmen decided to work all day and into the night without stopping. They wanted the children to be warm in the morning. So God answered the children's second prayer and there were some very happy and cosy boys and girls in Bristol!

And here's another amazing story about George Müller and prayer. As if George and Henry didn't have enough to do being responsible for thousands of children over the years, they also bought and distributed Bibles and New Testaments in order that the people to whom they were given could read God's Word and come to faith in Jesus. In answer to prayer, God provided them with the money to buy 285,407 Bibles, 1,459,506 New Testaments and 244,351 other Christian leaflets and books which were all given away!

God doesn't do miracles just to give us what we want when we want it. But he does hear and answer every single believing prayer. Sometimes his answer is 'yes'. Sometimes his answer is 'no', when we ask for what is not good or right. And sometimes, really quite often, God's answer is 'not yet', when we ask for something before the Lord wants us to have it. The wonderful thing is that when we grow up and look back over the years, we can see that even when God's answer was 'no' or 'not yet' he was absolutely right.

THE EXACT TIME

About the time George Müller moved to Bristol a baby boy was born in Barnsley, Yorkshire. His name was Hudson Taylor and he became a Christian in a remarkable way. His parents were Christians and Hudson knew about Jesus from before he could remember. But by the time he was seventeen he had not asked Jesus to be his Saviour although his young sister, Amelia, had.

Once his mother was away for a time visiting and Hudson was at home. He was mooching around looking for something to do when he picked up a Christian booklet called a tract. Tracts were written to tell people about Jesus. They usually started with an interesting story and then went on to a sermon. Hudson decided that he would read the interesting story but miss out on the sermon! However, God had other plans and the teenager read through the

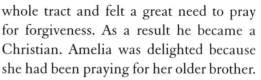

whole tract and felt a great need to pray for forgiveness. As a result he became a Christian. Amelia was delighted because she had been praying for her older brother.

At exactly the same time, fifty miles away, Hudson's mother was praying for his conversion. And when her son trusted in Jesus, she knew in her heart that her prayer had been answered and so her prayer changed. She started to praise God that her boy was now a believer! Meanwhile, back in Barnsley, Hudson told Amelia what had happened and made her promise not to write to tell their mother. He wanted to tell her the good news himself. However, when Mrs Taylor arrived home two weeks later she already knew! Hudson thought that his sister had broken her promise until his mother explained what had happened. A little while later Hudson picked up a notebook that belonged to his sister, thinking it was one of his own, and he read these words, 'I will pray every day for Hudson's conversion.' Hudson learned a lesson that day. Prayer is powerful because God hears his people and answers them.

In 1853, when he was twenty-one years old, Hudson Taylor went as a missionary to China. He had known about China all of his life because his dad was fascinated by all things Chinese, especially how the people of that great country could be taught about Jesus. Much of China was closed to foreigners when he went. But by 1865 the laws had changed and missionaries could get into parts of the country that had formerly been closed. Hudson prayed a very bold prayer. He prayed that God would send twenty-four more missionaries to China so that the gospel could be spread. That was how the China Inland Mission began, and the first sixteen CIM missionaries set sail the next year on a ship called the *Lammermuir.*

Eight years later, Hudson Taylor was once again praying for people. He actually wrote in his Bible what his prayer was and dated it. So we know that it was on 27th January 1874 that he asked God for one hundred Chinese Christian missionaries to take the good news about Jesus to places where he was completely unknown. Then he thanked God and prayed for strength of body, wisdom of mind and grace of soul to do his work.

Just after that it seemed as if God had not answered Hudson's prayer. For, instead of having strength of body, he became seriously ill. Not only that, he didn't have enough money to pay workers to go to new places. Hudson decided to write to Christians in London explaining the problem. Some time later, when he was keeping better, a letter arrived from England. It was from a man who had never been in touch before.

'My dear Sir,' it read, 'I bless God that in two months I hope to be able to send you £800 to be used for work in new areas.' Hudson knew that this was God's answer to his prayer. And he was especially thrilled that the letter had taken so long to come from England that it had actually been written before he prayed the prayer he had written in his Bible. God not only hears and answers prayer, he sometimes answers before the prayers are even prayed!

The following year Hudson Taylor was back in England travelling around the country telling people about China. Once, in a railway station on his way home, he met up with a man who knew about the work and they boarded the train together. The man said that he'd like to give some money for the China Inland Mission and he took a £50 note from his wallet. That was a HUGE amount of money! It still is.

'Did you not mean to give me five pounds?' asked Hudson, realising that the man had made a mistake.

His fellow traveller looked surprised.

'I cannot take it back. Five pounds was what I meant to give, but God must have intended you to have fifty. I cannot take it back.'

That night, when Hudson arrived home, he discovered that everyone in the house was in one room praying. There was an urgent need in China and they were praying for enough money to meet it. The fifty pound note that Hudson carried in his pocket was enough to meet that need. Hudson's fellow traveller was absolutely right when he said that God intended him to have fifty for that was exactly what was needed!

By the early 1880s, CIM had over a hundred missionaries, but Hudson and his fellow workers began to pray for another seventy new missionaries by 1884. After they prayed, someone said how good it would be if they could meet in 1884 to thank God for the seventy he would send. Another man thought differently. He was so sure that God would answer their prayers that he said they should have their special thank-you service there and then. That's what they did. And seventy new missionaries did arrive before the date they had set.

As CIM grew the work expanded and more and more people were needed. By 1886 Hudson and the others were praying for another hundred to be sent out in 1887! They even made up a prayer song that they sang together at every meal.

> Oh send the hundred workers, Lord,
> Those of thy heart and mind and choice,
> To tell thy love both far and wide –
> So shall we praise thee and rejoice;
> And above the rest this note shall swell,
> My Jesus has done all things well.

Before the end of 1887, 102 more missionaries set sail for China. Three years later CIM began praying for 1,000 new men and women to join the work!

By the time Hudson Taylor died in 1905 and went home to Jesus in heaven, there were 825 CIM missionaries serving in over 300 different parts of that great country. CIM is now part of OMF International, a large mission that reaches out to twelve different countries in East Asia (including China) with the good news that Jesus saves.

When we pray, we just can't begin to imagine how God might answer. Think about Amelia. She prayed for her brother to become a Christian ... and look at all that followed from his conversion!

HONEST JOHN

John Galt was an honest man. How do I know he was honest? Here's how. He moved from Scotland to London and found a job in a draper's shop. When the time for a sale came round, the man who owned the shop put a notice in his window saying that towels were being sold for half-price. But John knew that wasn't true! A lady came into the shop, looked John in the eyes and said, 'These towels are being sold at half price, are they not?' For a minute he didn't know what to say. Then he answered, 'Madam, this is what the head of this department has to say about these towels.' John Galt was so honest that he left his job rather than tell a lie.

I'm telling you that story so that you will know to believe an account John gave of what happened one bitterly cold winter when he was working as a London City Missionary. The area he worked in was

71

called Poplar and some of the people were very poor indeed. Fewer than half of the men and women could read and write. Men mostly found work for just one day at a time in the docks and if there was no work, there was no money at the end of the day.

Imagine such a freezing cold winter that the great River Thames froze solid at Poplar. So deep and hard was the ice that horses were able to cross over. For two whole months the temperature didn't rise enough to melt the river. That was terrible news for the day workers at the docks. For, if the river was frozen over, ships couldn't get up to the docks. And if ships couldn't get in, there were no cargos to load and unload. That meant no jobs. No jobs meant no money, and no money meant no food.

One day when John was visiting a home in Poplar, he discovered that the family there had nothing to eat, no fuel to heat their home and very little clothing. Two young boys had their feet tied in rags because they didn't have shoes and their mother's clothes hardly covered her. The boys crouched close together on a straw mattress to try to keep each other warm. The mother held a tiny baby that was crying with cold. The poor father was ill with exhaustion and lack of food as he tramped round the streets looking for work. There was none. John knew of fifty families who were just as desperate.

John Galt went home and told his wife all about it. They had only seventy-four pence in their possession, but they agreed to use it to buy bread for the fifty families. The missionary and his wife prayed, not just a 'God bless the poor people' prayer, more a 'crying out to God to provide' prayer. They pleaded to God to help the families who were in such awful need. That afternoon John continued his visiting. Meanwhile Mrs Galt wrote four letters to friends to whom she should have been writing anyway. She didn't beg for money, but she did explain how desperate the people of Poplar were and that she and her husband had no more money to use to help them. The next morning, while the Galts were having their breakfast, the postman came to the door. Two of the friends Mrs Galt had written to had sent money right away. Between them they sent seventy-five pence, one pence more than the Galts had spent on bread!

That day John found a further twenty-five families who were just as needy and ordered seventy-five loaves to stop them starving. God heard and answered the Galts' prayers and the following morning the postman brought enough money to buy bread for all seventy-five families. Day after day the ice on the Thames grew thicker and men walked the street in a useless attempt to find work. Day after day John Galt

walked the streets too, looking for more starving families to add to his list. And day after day God answered their prayers, providing money to buy one loaf for each of these families. The days became weeks and still the freeze went on and still God gave what was needed. No more letters were written after the original four.

One day, nearly three weeks from the beginning of this story, a letter came from one of the ladies who had replied on the very first day. She said that she had heard how terrible the continuing situation in Poplar was and felt ashamed that she had sent so little. The kind woman finished with, 'I have pleasure in enclosing double the first amount.' But there was a problem; the woman had forgotten to put her money in the envelope! John and his wife didn't chase her up, rather they waited to see how God would solve the problem. And they prayed.

The following morning brought splendid news. There was a letter from that woman with her money PLUS an extra three guineas from her husband and son-in-law! You probably won't have heard of guineas, but three would then have equalled £3.15. That was enough to buy 210 loaves of bread in those days! No more money came in after that. John and his wife used it to feed the families they knew were most in need. Of course, as no more money came in, they had less left each day. Then when there was no money left to buy food for the hungry, the ice on the great River Thames at Poplar thawed enough to allow ships in and out and all the men went back to work. Just imagine the joyful thank-you prayers John Galt and his wife prayed that day! And if you think that story is too fantastic to be true, remember what you discovered at the beginning – Honest John would rather lose his job than tell a lie!

When we see people in need we, like John and his wife, should pray that God will give them what they need. But there's an interesting little twist in the story and I wonder if you noticed it. On the first day when John saw that starving couple with their two little boys and baby and realised the terrible need, he didn't only pray and expect God to answer, he also used his own money to help. Asking God to help is not an excuse for not helping ourselves.

ANSWER TO THE TALKING DRUM

How do you get students to come to a nursing course you are planning to run in the middle of a jungle, in the middle of the Democratic Republic of Congo, right in the middle of Africa? You do two things. You pray to God about it and you send a message by the talking drum.

There was certainly plenty of prayer. Dr Helen Roseveare, an English missionary doctor, had been given the job of starting a nurses' training course for young men at a mission station called Nyankunde. The vision was that those trained there would help to set up a medical service to care for the people of the northeast of the country, all a quarter of a million miles of it. You don't take on a job like that without prayer.

But what's all this about a talking drum? Well, there were no landline telephones, no cell phones and no Internet, but there was an efficient method

of communication, the talking drum. Someone would beat out a rhythm on the drum so that people could hear it for miles around. That was the way news spread around the area. This time a message was sent out saying that any young men who had basic primary school education, and who wanted to train as nurses should come to Nyankunde on a certain date. Mama Luka (that was Dr Roseveare's Congolese name) had plenty to do before that date came. She had to decide what to teach her students. And she had to work out how to tell them that there was no hospital, no nurses' training college and nowhere for her students to stay. In other words, she had a whole lot of praying to do!

The day came and so did twenty-two young men. Girls didn't nurse in the Congo at that time; nurses were male. All that existed of the nursing school was a small table and a chair. Mama Luka sat on the chair, at the table, and spoke to each of the young men. Then she sent them to John Mangadima, her Congolese associate, who gave them all they needed. Each received a plate, mug and spoon, soap, a lamp and matches and a blanket in which to wrap up at night.

Picture the scene. There is Mama Luka sitting at her table, a list of names in front of her. There is John Mangadima handing out supplies.

'Where's the nursing school?' the bravest of the young men asked.

Mama Luka waved her hand vaguely in the direction of an area of elephant grass[4]. 'Over there,' she told them.

'Where are the dormitories?' asked another, who was beginning to be suspicious.

'Over there,' announced Mama Luka, pointing towards the elephant grass once more.

A light was dawning in twenty-two confused faces as the fact that there was no nursing school and there were no dormitories sank in.

John Mangadima called out the boys' names.

'I will show you where to sleep,' he told them, as he led them to the primary school.

'I'm not sleeping in there!' one announced.

Another was very indignant. 'We've finished with primary school! This is an insult!'

'I wouldn't have come if I'd thought it would be like this,' one said crossly, as he stomped after John Mangadima.

Mama Luka remained behind. And what did she do? She prayed … hard.

That afternoon she was back at her table and chair when the would-be students

---

[4] If elephant grass isn't called that because it's so high, it should be.

returned, not looking best pleased. Once again the doctor prayed. What happened in the next hour was hugely important.

'Ready?' she asked. 'Let's go!'

Off they went – the doctor, John Mangadima, and twenty-two young men through elephant grass higher than they were, through mud that stuck to their feet and through brambles that scratched as they passed. Up and up they climbed until they were at the top of a hill. Somewhere along the way Mama Luka's prayer began to be answered. The stomping turned into strolling and the humping into happy laughter as they began to relax and enjoy themselves. By the time they reached the top of the hill the doctor was saying thank-you to her heavenly Father.

'Look down the valley,' Mama Luka told them, when the last of the young men reached the top.

'That's the nursing school,' she said, pointing to an area on which there was no building at all. 'And those are the dormitories,' she said, indicating another area of elephant grass.

The boys stared at each other and then at the doctor. She looked from one to another, meeting each set of eyes fairly and squarely.

'You build,' she told them. 'I teach.' Mama Luka then explained her plan. They (that was the boys with her help) would fell trees, drag them from the jungle and then use them to build the walls of the nursing school and dormitories. They would gather material for thatch and construct the roofs. 'And when that's all done,' she concluded, 'I'll teach you everything you need to know to be nurses and health workers.'

You can imagine the reactions she saw in the circle of faces.

'I'll meet you at 6.30 tomorrow morning and you can tell me your decision then.'

That night Dr Helen Roseveare took the whole situation to God in prayer. John Mangadima prayed. All the Christians in the compound prayed. Much prayer went from Nyankunde to heaven in the dark night hours. The following morning no one but the doctor was there on time. She waited and prayed and got soaked in the rain. It was after 8.30 when they arrived, all twenty-two of them. They weren't the happiest young men, but they agreed to her plan. Mama Luka's prayers were answered.

The young men did cut down trees and drag them out of the jungle. They did build the nurses' school and their dormitories, all with their doctor's help. Mama Luka didn't ask them to do what she wasn't prepared to try herself. And she kept her side of the agreement. When all the building work was done – including a football pitch where her students could enjoy themselves

81

– she trained them to be nurses. It took a long time, but eventually the nursing school at Nyankunde was recognised by the Congolese government! And it all started with two very different means of communication – prayer and talking drums.

As the students built the nursing school, they knew that the doctor was praying and they saw her prayers being answered in their lives. When we look at our lives, we can see other people's prayers being answered in us.

GRANDFATHER FEDOR

Dimitry Mustafin was a little boy in Russia in the 1950s. Russia was then a Communist country and many things that we think are ordinary were forbidden by law. For example, it was illegal to read the Bible and to tell children about the Lord Jesus. People were put in prison just for being Christians and sadly many of them were killed.

Of course, because it was against the law to teach about Christ, there was no Christmas in Communist times. Instead they celebrated New Year with decorated trees and presents. Only once was 'Christmas' celebrated at Dimitry's school, but it was celebrated in such a way as to teach that the birth of Jesus was nonsense. It was shown as a joke with silly shepherds leaving their sheep to go astray, and stupid 'wise' men travelling miles on camels to see a baby! At school Dimitry was taught that Jesus was the hero of a

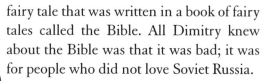

fairy tale that was written in a book of fairy tales called the Bible. All Dimitry knew about the Bible was that it was bad; it was for people who did not love Soviet Russia.

However, God is much more powerful and wonderful than Communism and, for all that Dimitry was taught in school, he became a Christian in 1986, when he was working for a year in Italy. By then he was grown up and a university professor. When he returned to Russia he broke the law by taking Bibles (forbidden books!) with him into the country. It was when Dimitry gave one as a gift to his mother that she told him the story of his own family that he had not known before.

In 1936 many Christian churches were closed. The Bible was said to be dangerous and lots of believers were put in prison, among them Dimitry's Grandfather Fedor. Fedor was honest and peaceful, friendly and kind. But he was a Christian and the Government believed him to be a danger to Communist society. Grandfather Fedor was taken to prison and killed as a criminal. He died with words from the Bible on his lips. As he died he was praying for his executors.

Four years after Dimitry became a Christian, Communism fell in Russia and it was once again legal to own and read the Bible, to teach and preach about Jesus. Dimitry and some of his Christian friends began distributing Bibles and New Testaments in schools, prisons, hospitals and other places too. Butirka Prison was just across the road from the university in which Dimitry was a professor and he went there so often that the prison governor came to know him and like him. That was why, when Victory Day came around, he was invited to a special meal in the prison. Victory Day is when Russians honour elderly and retired people who have served the country in their work or in the armed forces.

There was a delicious meal that evening and Dimitry enjoyed it very much. Then there was a concert and he enjoyed that too. After the concert was over Colonel Alexander Volkov, the Governor of Butirka Prison, said he had someone he wanted Dimitry to meet. That someone was a very old man.

'Dimitry, I want to introduce you to a very special man. He is our honoured veteran. He worked in the prison for thirty years as … an … executioner.'

Colonel Alexander Volkov said the words very slowly and quietly, and then he showed Dimitry an old, skinny man with a red face and small eyes, who was in his eighties. It had been his job to kill people, and among his victims might have been Dimitry's Grandfather Fedor, who was killed in Butirka because he was a Christian.

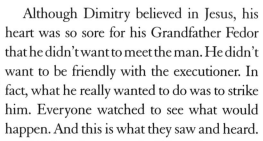

Although Dimitry believed in Jesus, his heart was so sore for his Grandfather Fedor that he didn't want to meet the man. He didn't want to be friendly with the executioner. In fact, what he really wanted to do was to strike him. Everyone watched to see what would happen. And this is what they saw and heard.

Dimitry always carried New Testaments with him and he gave one to the old man.

'I know that I am a terrible sinner,' said the old man. 'But how can I be forgiven by the Lord?'

Dimitry told him (and everyone else who was listening) about the two criminals who were crucified at the same time as Jesus, and about one of them praying just before he died.

'Please, pray for me,' asked the ex-executioner.

'No,' Dimitry answered immediately. He was so upset about Grandfather Fedor that he didn't want to pray for the man. 'A prayer is a conversation with the Lord. You have to pray by yourself.'

'I do not know any prayer,' said the ex-executioner. 'Teach me how to pray. Please, lead me in a prayer.'

So it was that Dimitry was forced to pray the hardest prayer of his life. He closed his eyes but was not able to open his mouth. With closed lips he asked the Lord to come into his heart and fill it with love. Then Dimitry started to pray about himself because he realised that he needed to be forgiven for how he was feeling. He started to pray loudly, and then heard the old man repeating the words of his prayer word by word and asking God to forgive him. Dimitry asked the Lord to bring peace into the ex-executioner's life and forgive him, to become his Saviour and Protector. He asked the Lord to be with that old man always.

When Dimitry finished praying he saw that the executioner was crying. His eyes were full of tears, but he looked happy. Then the old man shook Dimitry's hand, gave him a hug and kissed him. Dimitry has never seen that man again, but he knows that even an executioner can be saved and go to heaven when he dies, for God is so wonderful and gracious that he saves all who call out to him. Dimitry hopes that when he goes to heaven he will meet that old man once more and meet Grandfather Fedor too.

Sadly, there are still countries in the world where people are put in prison, and even killed, for believing in Jesus. Pray for them.

THE BOY AND THE WITCHDOCTOR

Not every nurse likes all kinds of nursing. Georgie Orme, a nurse from Edinburgh in Scotland, didn't like nursing children. In fact, she really didn't like working with children at all. You might wonder why she trained to be a midwife and bring new babies into the world. Well, although she just loved helping babies to be born, she was quite happy to then give them to their mothers to take home!

Some time after Georgie became a Christian she felt sure that God wanted her to go to Bible college and train to be a missionary. It was towards the end of her time there that what seemed like a very odd thing happened. A minister came to visit the college.

'I asked the Lord to give me a Scripture verse for each one of you,' he told the students. 'I have written beside each name the verse I believe the Lord has given me for you. During the course of the day I will

call each of you into my room and give you your verse.'

When Georgie was called in, the verse she was given was 1 Thessalonians 2: 7-8.

> We were gentle among you like a mother caring for her little children. We loved you so much that we were delighted to share with you not only the gospel of God but our lives as well because you had become so dear to us.

'This is for you,' the man said, 'because the ministry I believe God is saying you will have is a caring one, where your care isn't just a job. You will share your life with those you are caring for, just as in a family where the mother cares for her children.'

Now, Georgie had prayed that God would show her what he wanted her to do, but that wasn't really the answer she was looking for. Remember, she didn't really like working with children very much!

First of all Georgie Orme went to Uganda and then, shortly afterwards, to Kenya. When she arrived there she was poorly and was cared for by two missionaries called Lorna Eglin and Betty Allcock at the Child Care Centre at Kajiado. It was when she was there that Georgie was shown the job that God wanted her to do. Lorna and Betty needed someone to help them with their work and they were sure that Georgie was just the right person.

God gathered a little group of people at Kajiado and used them to completely change the lives of some terribly disabled boys and girls. He brought Lorna and Betty from South Africa to Kajiado and Georgie all the way from Scotland. Another member of the team was Rebecca and she was from the north of Kenya. Rebecca had been married to a witchdoctor but, when they had no children, her husband treated her so cruelly that she ran away. Her sister, who was loving and kind and had children of her own, said that when she had another baby she would give it to Rebecca to care for as her own. That's what happened. A little boy was born and given to Rebecca. By the time Georgie arrived at Kajiado, Rebecca was a house-mother in the Child Care Centre and the boys and girls loved her. She loved them too, but she loved the Lord Jesus most of all.

When visiting a hospital, Lorna and Betty met a boy called Ntuyoto. He had suffered from a disease called polio that left him very disabled and they wanted him to come to the Centre to be helped. Georgie was sent to find him. With a great deal of difficulty she eventually arrived at his village where she found Ntuyoto on the ground pulling himself along by his arms and dragging thin, floppy, spidery legs behind him through dirt and dust and cow dung. Ntuyoto's dad loved his little

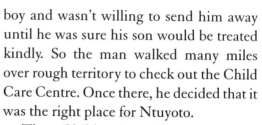

boy and wasn't willing to send him away until he was sure his son would be treated kindly. So the man walked many miles over rough territory to check out the Child Care Centre. Once there, he decided that it was the right place for Ntuyoto.

The Child Care Centre was a wonderful place where children who had suffered from polio could have calipers made for them to help them walk. Treatment began right away with Georgie and others working on Ntuyoto's useless legs for hours at a time. Eventually Ntuyoto was measured and calipers made to keep his legs straight. Then his real work began. It took a long, long time; it took a lot of exercises. It took hard, hard work, but ... eventually ... the great day came when Ntuyoyo took his very first steps! Georgie was there when he walked that day and she heard him saying something over and over again. Listening carefully, she heard the words, 'Ashe Yesu! Ashe Yesu! Ashe Yesu!' Translated into English that means, 'Thank you, Jesus!' over and over again.

Rebecca was Ntuyoto's housemother and every night as she had helped the boy to bed she prayed with him, asking Jesus to enable him to walk. So it was that, on the day he took his first steps, brave Ntuyoto knew who to thank. But Rebecca didn't only pray for the boys and girls in her care, she also prayed for the cruel old witchdoctor who was her husband.

One day Georgie saw the witchdoctor coming along the road. She was not best pleased as he was one of her least favourite people. He had one leg shorter than the other and could be recognized from quite a long distance. Georgie's heart sank. In the tradition of that part of Kenya witchdoctors, they are called oloibonis, have no land of their own. Instead they have to be given somewhere to stay wherever they go. This particular oloiboni was such a bad-tempered growl of a man that he kept having to move to somewhere new after he'd fallen out with whoever he was staying with. When that happened he expected Georgie to help move all his gourds, bones and witchdoctory powders and potions to another village. That was one job she just hated doing!

Despite his cruelty, Rebecca still prayed for her husband. God in his great goodness heard her prayer and one day her husband asked Jesus to forgive his sins and to be his Saviour! Rebecca was so thrilled! All the missionaries, including a very pleased Georgie, and the local preachers gathered together that day and had a burial service at which all the evil powders and potions and bones were laid in a grave of cow dung. The gourds that had held them were put into a cattle enclosure where they would be broken to pieces, ground down to dust and trampled into the earth.

God hears every prayer and answers each one. Sometimes God's answer is 'no', sometimes it's 'yes' and sometimes it's 'not yet'. Whatever God's answer is, it's the right one for he only does what is good. All the people in this book either prayed or were prayed for. Do you pray? If you do, remember to look for answers and to thank God for them. If you don't yet pray, God is waiting to hear from you. And remember, the only way to learn to pray … is to pray!

BOOKS BY IRENE HOWAT

ON FIRE

Each of these stories is about fire – but there's not a matchstick or a marshmallow in sight! They are all from the Bible and show how God has used fire throughout scripture in a variety of ways. He used fire to get Moses to pay attention. He used it to help the Israelites find their way through the dark. He used it to keep Adam and Eve out of the garden. But fire also appears in the New Testament... soldiers with torches arrest Jesus in the garden of Gethsemane. Peter warms himself by some flames while at the same time he denies the Lord Jesus. Jesus himself cooks a fish Barbie on the beach after his resurrection and the Holy Spirit comes down on the disciples at Pentecost with tongues of flame.

ISBN: 978-1-84550-780-0

BOOKS ABLAZE

There are some bonfires in this book. Books were amongst some of the things set alight during church history. In fact flames were used to persecute Christians throughout church history. Their possessions and homes were set alight. Christians were even killed and burned for their faith. But there was one fire that didn't happen - on the 5th of November, 1605 Guy Fawkes and others decided to set fire to the Houses of Parliament in the United Kingdom. Irene Howat tells the Christian story behind this and other incidents in history. You will see how not even fire or the plans of evil men can separate Christians from the love of God.

ISBN: 978-1-84550-781-7

CHRISTIAN FOCUS PUBLICATIONS

Christian Focus | Christian Heritage | CF4K | Mentor

Christian Focus Publications publishes books for adults and children under its four main imprints: Christian Focus, CF4K, Mentor and Christian Heritage. Our books reflect our conviction that God's Word is reliable and Jesus is the way to know him, and live for ever with him.

Our children's publication list includes a Sunday School curriculum that covers pre-school to early teens, and puzzle and activity books. We also publish personal and family devotional titles, biographies and inspirational stories that children will love.

If you are looking for quality Bible teaching for children then we have an excellent range of Bible stories and age-specific theological books.

From pre-school board books to teenage apologetics, we have it covered!

Find us at our web page:
www.christianfocus.com

CF4 •K
Because you're never too young to know Jesus